CW00518762

MICROWAVE DRIED FRUIT
& OTHER FRUIT DELICACIES

· Isabel Webb ·

The Five Mile Press

The Five Mile Press
351 Whitehorse Road
Balwyn Victoria 3103

First published 1991

Copyright © text Isabel Webb
Copyright © illustrations The Five Mile Press Pty Ltd

All rights reserved. No part of this publication may
be reproduced, stored in a retrieval system, or
transmitted in any form or by any means,
electronic, mechanical photocopying, recording or
otherwise without the prior written permission of
the Publishers.

Design: Geoff Hocking
Illustrations: Margie Chellew
Photography: Neil Lorimer
Production: Emma Borghesi
Typeset by Post Typesetters, Brisbane, Qld
Printed in Singapore by Kyodo Printing Co. Ltd

National Library of Australia
Cataloguing-in-Publication data

Webb, Isabel, 1936- .
Microwave dried fruit & other fruit delicacies.

Includes index.
ISBN 0-86788-400-2
ISBN 0-86788-385-5 (pbk.).

1. Fruit — Preservation. 2. Microwave cookery.
I. Title.

541.4

This book may be ordered by mail from the Publisher.
Please add $2.50 for postage and handling for each copy
But try your bookshop first!

Preface

How lovely it is when your favourite fruits are in season and readily available! But sometimes the abundance can be overwhelming, and good ideas for using them all not exactly forthcoming.

My first book, *Microwave Bottling*, introduced the microwave method of preserving fruit, jellies, jams, pickles and sauces. My second, *Low-sugar Microwave Bottling*, showed how to preserve all of these with minimal — or, in some cases, no — added sugar. In this book I now suggest many other wonderful fruit recipes that prevent waste and enable you to stock up for the leaner seasons.

I have included a quick, easy way of drying your own fruit — marvellous for mueslis, snacks and fruit compotes — and simple methods of making glacé fruit and fruit liqueurs, all in the microwave. Also included are recipes for refreshing fruit sorbets, fruit fillings, delicious fruity ice-creams and some very special jams and chutneys.

This wide variety of ideas is proof of the natural versatility of fruit and the practical convenience of the microwave oven.

Contents

$\mathcal{A}$ Word About Microwaves

- Make sure there's no excess water on the microwave carousel.
- Remember that every microwave oven is slightly different, and power supplies can vary, especially at peak times or when several appliances are being run from the same circuit. The cooking times will prove more accurate if you clean and dry the microwave carousel before you start. Any moisture will use up microwave energy and could affect cooking time.

Settings

HIGH = 100 per cent microwaves
MEDIUM-HIGH = 75 per cent microwaves
MEDIUM = 50 per cent microwave
DEFROST = 30 per cent microwaves

Chapter 1

Home-dried Fruit

Dried fruit has the same nutritional value and fibre content as fresh fruit, but in a concentrated form. The microwave drying process is simple and quick, and particularly appeals to people who are sensitive or allergic to the chemicals used in most commercial drying methods. Fruit dried in your microwave is ready for use the same day or may be stored for later.

The Purpose of Drying Food

The drying process removes excess moisture from food. This inhibits the growth of moulds and enzymes that would normally cause deterioration over a period of time, and thus enables the food to be stored.

In the past, food was dried in the sun or in a low-temperature oven, taking many hours or even days. The slowness of the process put a lot of people off. But now, with the wonderful invention of the microwave oven, food can be oven-dried in a matter of minutes, making the process more appealing to a greater number of people.

The times given in this book are for a 650-watt microwave oven. However, because of variations in microwave ovens, conditions, and the size and texture of the fruit itself, the times are a guide only; you may need to add or subtract a few seconds or minutes, just as you do in any sort of cooking.

Suitable Fruits

The most popular and most suitable fruits for microwave drying are apricots, bananas, apples, figs, kiwi fruit (Chinese gooseberries), blue plums (prunes) and small grapes. Fruit used should be of first grade quality, ripe and without blemishes.

Preventing Discolouration

To prevent discolouration during the drying process, all peeled fruit (such as apples and bananas) should first be washed and soaked in lemon water — a solution of 2 cups water and the juice of 1 lemon (approximately 3 tablespoons) — for 15–20 minutes and patted dry.

Alternatively, you can soak them in brine — a solution of 60 g (2 oz) salt in 1.5 (3 pints) litres water — for 15–20 minutes. Then rinse in cold water and pat dry on a clean cloth.

Testing the Fruit

On removal from the oven, the fruit should be dry to the touch, pliable and rubbery in texture, and, if pressed between two fingers, should recover its original bulk when released. If the right results are not achieved, return the fruit to the microwave for further drying for about 5–10 minutes on DEFROST; then re-test.

Standing and Storing Dried Fruit

Once removed from the oven, the fruit should be allowed to dry on a cake cooler or wire rack for a further 12–24 hours before being stored.

Dried fruit does not last forever. However, providing it is properly dried and stored, it will retain its optimum flavour and colour for 3–5 months and may last up to 6 months. Store dried fruit in loosely covered jars, tins or paper-lined boxes, or in plastic storage bags tied at the top and punctured with 1 or 2 tiny holes. The containers should not be airtight, as the fruit will sweat. Place in a cool, dry, well-ventilated place. If mould forms, this means the fruit has not been dried properly and should be discarded.

*Do*s and *Don't*s

The following is a checklist of the main *do*s and *don't*s of microwave fruit drying:

- If possible choose fruits in season for best results.
- Always wash fruit thoroughly before beginning.
- Prevent discolouration by bleaching fruit in lemon water or brine before drying.
- Inspect the fruit towards the end of the drying time and remove any pieces that are ready before others.
- Dry the fruit longer than the specified time if necessary but don't overdry it.
- Don't use fruit that is damaged or bruised or markedly under-ripe. It will lose shape and dry unevenly. Note that drying cannot improve the food; it only enables longer storage.
- Don't leave excess water on the carousel or the washed fruit — always dry with a clean cloth before beginning.
- Don't use paper towelling on the carousel. Brown or white kitchen paper or butcher's paper is ideal.
- Don't stack or cram fruit whilst drying — always spread in a single layer, not touching, to avoid burning and produce more even results and fewer variations in drying time.
- Don't slice fruit too thickly as the drying times given are for suggested sizes, and thicker or bigger pieces will not dry successfully in the given times.

Apples

1 Peel and core 2 medium-sized apples. Cut into approximately 10 slices, 5 mm (¼ in) thick.

2 Soak in lemon water to prevent discolouration (see page 9).

3 Drain and pat dry.

4 Cut a circle of brown or white kitchen paper to fit the carousel.

5 Arrange apple slices in a single layer on the paper, making sure they don't touch each other.

6 Set microwave on DEFROST and dry for 35–45 minutes or until dry and rubbery to touch (see page 10).

7 Stand and store according to directions on page 10.

Apricots

1 Choose 16–18 firm, ripe, unblemished apricots. Wash.

2 Cut in halves and remove stones.

3 Soak in lemon water to prevent discolouration (see page 9).

4 Drain and pat dry.

5 Place directly onto carousel in a single layer with cut side facing down, making sure they don't touch each other.

6 Set microwave on DEFROST and dry for 50–60 minutes or until they have shrivelled to about half their size and are dry and rubbery to touch (see page 10).

7   Stand and store according to directions on page 10.

Bananas

1   Peel 2 firm, ripe bananas under running water to help prevent discolouration. Remove any blemishes.

2   Slice into circles 5 mm (¼ in) thick (approximately 30–40 slices).

3   Soak in lemon water to prevent discolouration (see page 9).

4   Drain and pat dry.

5   Cut a circle of brown or white kitchen paper to fit the carousel.

6   Arrange slices in a single layer on the paper, making sure they don't touch each other.

7   Set microwave on DEFROST and dry for 35–45 minutes or until dry and rubbery to touch (see page 10).

8   Stand and store according to directions on page 10.

Figs

1 Choose 15–20 ripe, unblemished figs. Wash.

2 Cut in halves if large; or leave whole, cutting away the stem.

3 Arrange halved fruit cut side down directly on carousel in a single layer, or distribute whole fruit evenly, making sure they don't touch each other.

4 Set microwave on DEFROST and dry for 35–45 minutes or until dry and rubbery to touch (see page 10).

5 Stand and store according to directions on page 10.

Grapes

1 Choose 50-60 fresh, unblemished grapes.

2 Remove stalks, wash and pat dry.

3 Cut a circle of brown or white kitchen paper to fit the carousel.

4 Spread grapes evenly in a single layer on the paper, making sure they don't touch each other.

5 Set microwave on DEFROST and dry for 50-60 minutes, moving grapes about on the paper 2-3 times while drying. When ready the grapes will be about half their original size and sticky to touch.

6 Stand and store according to directions on page 10.

Kiwi Fruit

1 Choose 4 ripe and unblemished kiwi fruit and remove skins.

2 Slice into circles 5 mm (¼ in) thick (approximately 20 slices).

3 Cut a circle of brown or white kitchen paper to fit the carousel.

4 Arrange slices in a single layer on the paper making sure they don't touch each other.

5 Set microwave on DEFROST and dry for 20-30 minutes or until dry and rubbery to touch (see page 10).

6 Stand and store according to directions on page 10.

Mangoes

1 Choose 2 or 3 medium-sized firm and ripe mangoes.

2 Remove skin by scoring vertically at intervals and peeling down from stem. The skin will come away easily if the fruit is ripe.

3 Cut into 10-mm (½-in) wedges by cutting with a knife down onto the seed and easing each segment away.

4 Cut a circle of brown or white kitchen paper to fit the carousel.

5 Arrange wedges in a single layer on the paper making sure they don't touch each other.

6 Set microwave on DEFROST and dry for 40-50 minutes or until wedges have shrivelled to three-quarters of their original size and are slightly sticky to touch.

7 Stand and store according to directions on page 10.

Dried Honey Mango

1 For every mango allow 2 teaspoons honey.

2 Heat honey in a microwave-proof bowl for 30 seconds.

3 Pour over mango wedges prepared by following steps 2-3 of previous recipe. Toss lightly to coat mangoes with honey.

4 Dry as in steps 4-7 of previous recipe.

Fruit dried in your microwave is free of chemicals,
— unlike most commercially-processed dried fruit.

*Start the day with home-made muesli (page 21)
or fruit compote (page 21).*

Peaches

1 Choose 3 or 4 medium-sized, yellow-fleshed, firm and ripe peaches.

2 Peel and cut into 10–mm (½–in) wedges by cutting with a knife down onto the stone and easing each segment away.

3 Arrange wedges directly on carousel, making sure they don't touch each other.

4 Set microwave on DEFROST and dry for 30–40 minutes or until wedges have shrivelled to three-quarters of their original size and are dry to touch.

5 Stand and store according to directions on page 10.

Pineapple

1   Choose a ripe pineapple. To do this turn the pineapple upside-down and smell the base where the fruit was joined to the bush. If there is no smell it isn't ripe and if it smells mouldy it is over-ripe. When it's just right, it will have a fresh, fruity aroma.

2   Peel, eye and core pineapple.

3   Cut into 5-mm (¼-in) slices (approximately 18-24), halves or pieces.

4   Cut a circle of brown or white kitchen paper to fit the carousel.

5   Arrange pieces in a single layer on the paper, making sure they don't touch each other.

6   Set microwave on DEFROST and dry for 45-60 minutes or until dry to touch and rubbery.

7   Stand and store according to directions on page 10.

Plums

NOTE: This method is for blue plums (prunes). If you use other varieties the drying time will vary slightly depending on size.

1 Choose 15-20 firm, ripe, unblemished plums.

2 If large cut in halves and remove stones. If left whole, cut away stem or prick all over with a sterile darning needle to prevent skins from splitting.

3 Place directly onto carousel in a single layer with cut side facing down (or spread whole plums evenly), making sure they don't touch each other.

4 Set microwave on DEFROST and dry for 35-45 minutes or until fruit has reduced in size and is dry to touch (see page 10).

5 Stand and store according to directions on page 10.

Tomatoes

1 Choose firm, ripe tomatoes, e.g. mama mia, romano (egg-shaped), cherry or sweet bite (marble-sized).

2 Cut small tomatoes into halves (lengthwise if egg-shaped and small) or large tomatoes into 10-mm (½-in) slices.

3 Arrange directly on carousel in a single layer, cut side up, making sure they don't touch each other.

4 Set microwave on DEFROST and dry for approximately 25-45 minutes (the time varies according to ripeness and size) or until shrivelled and dry to touch.

5 Stand as directed on page 10.

6 Place in jar and cover with herbed olive oil (see following recipe).

7 Leave 3–4 weeks to allow flavours to develop.

8 Serve as a pre-dinner savoury on croutons or biscuits along with a selection of cheeses.

Herbed Olive Oil

Combine:
Olive oil, 1 cup
Dried garlic, 1 teaspoon
Dried oregano, 1 teaspoon
Salt, ½ teaspoon
Dried chilli (optional), 1

Using Dried Fruit at Breakfast

Dried fruit is particularly handy in breakfasts. It can be chopped and combined in homemade muesli, or cooked and served as a nourishing compote.

Natural Breakfast Muesli

Combine:

Rolled oats, 3 cups
Mixed dried fruits, 1 cup
Shredded coconut, ¼ cup
Nuts of your choice, ¼ cup

Store the muesli in a covered container. This is a healthy, energy-giving food that is delicious alone or combined with another breakfast cereal. Muesli can also be served with compote or fresh fruit.

Dried Fruit Compote

The moisture that was extracted during the drying process can be replaced by soaking the fruit, or cooking it in water or fruit juice. Sugar or other sweeteners may be added to taste immediately after cooking. Artificial sweetener can cause a bitter taste, but is less likely to do so if added after the fruit has cooled. Cooking the fruit with the sweetener is not recommended, as the fruit will be inclined to toughen.

Ingredients

Dried fruit, 200 g (6 oz)
Water or fruit juice, 1½–2 cups
Sweetener to taste

Cooking Method

Place fruit and water in a microwave-proof bowl, cover and cook on MEDIUM-HIGH until fruit is soft and tender (approximately 12–15 minutes). Cool and sweeten to taste.

Soaking Method

Soak fruit in water or fruit juice for 6–8 hours or overnight ready for breakfast.

Chapter 2

Glacé and Crystallised Fruit

Glacé and crystallised fruit can be bought ready-prepared, but tends to be rather expensive. The microwave method of glazing and crystallising is quick and effective, causing very little damage to colour, flavour, texture and nutritional content. The finished product makes an attractive decoration for desserts or a special treat with after-dinner coffee or liqueurs. A box of glacé or crystallised fruits makes a luxurious gift.

Suitable Fruits

Firm fruits such as apricots, grapes, peaches, plums and pineapple give the best results. Ginger and the peel or whole-fruit slices of citrus fruit are very successful. The fruit should be of top quality, ripe and without blemishes, and it should be firm. Soft fruits such as berries are not suitable as they tend to break up and go mushy during the cooking process.

Preparing the Fruit

Fruit to be glazed or crystallised whole should be pricked with a large, darning needle to allow the syrup to penetrate the skin. Larger fruits should be peeled and halved or quartered.

Storing the Fruit

Glacé or crystallised fruit should not be stored in airtight containers. The ideal means of storage is a small cardboard box lined with waxed paper and covered with a lid. Layers of fruit can thus be separated by sheets of waxed paper to prevent sticking. If glass jars are used, do not cover with lids as the fruit will go mouldy due to lack of ventilation. Place in a cool, dry, airy place, where it will keep for 6–12 months.

Syrup for Glazing

When making syrup, observe the following points for best results:
- If a sugar thermometer is used to confirm cooking times, the correct temperature is easily ascertained. However, if you do not have one of these, the next-best method is to test for 'pulling consistency'. After 1 or 2 minutes of boiling, drop a tablespoon of syrup into a cup of cold water. When the cooled syrup is

transparent and can be stretched a little without breaking, the desired temperature has been achieved.

- You must ensure that the syrup does not crystallise while being boiled. To do this, do not stir when you first add water to the sugar. At the next stage, ensure that every single grain of sugar is dissolved or removed as directed. Just one remaining grain of sugar will cause crystallisation and render your syrup useless.
- Once the syrup has reached its correct temperature or consistency try not to disturb unnecessarily when dunking fruit.
- It is not advisable to glaze different varieties of fruit in the same syrup as the individual flavour can be lost.

Ingredients

Water or cooking liquid from fruit, 60 ml (¼ cup)

Sugar, 250 g (1 cup)

Cream of tartar, ½ teaspoon

Method

1 Place sugar in a microwave-proof bowl, add water carefully so as not to disturb sugar. Do NOT stir.

2 Cover and heat on HIGH for 1–2 minutes, until just below boiling point.

3 Now stir to dissolve sugar fully. Use a damp pastry brush to brush away any grains of sugar around the sides of the bowl.

4 When satisfied that all sugar is dissolved and syrup is completely clear, stir in cream of tartar (this inhibits crystallisation).

5 Return to microwave and boil on HIGH for approximately 3 minutes, or until syrup has reached 104° C (220° F) on a sugar thermometer, or until syrup is of a light 'pulling consistency' when tested in cold water (See page 23).

Glazing the Fruit

1 Add the fruit to the hot syrup. Return to microwave and continue boiling until fruit is just tender but still holds its shape — approximately 1-2 minutes.

2 Remove the bowl from the microwave and allow fruit to stand in syrup until transparent (approximately 10-12 minutes).

3 Remove fruit and arrange on a cake cooler to drain away excess syrup.

4 Return uncovered bowl to microwave, set on HIGH and bring syrup back to boiling point (approximately 1-2 minutes).

5 Place each piece of fruit separately on a skewer or draining spoon and dunk into the hot syrup.

6 Allow excess syrup to drip away for a minute or so before drying in the microwave.

Drying the Glacé Fruit

1 Cut a circle of brown or white kitchen paper to fit the carousel.

2 Arrange fruit slices in a single layer on the paper, making sure they don't touch each other.

3 Set microwave on DEFROST and dry for 15–20 minutes or until slightly sticky.

4 Allow to stand on a cake cooler for 12 hours, then store according to directions on page 23.

NOTE: For 500-550-watt microwave ovens, approximately 10 minutes' extra drying time will be necessary. For 700-750-watt ovens, approximately 10 minutes' less drying time will be necessary.

Crystallising the Fruit

Glacé fruit is delicious, but some people prefer crystallised fruit. To make this, you simply take your glacé fruit and dunk it in boiling water. Then you toss it in granulated sugar until well-coated.

Apricots

Ingredients

Apricots, 10–12
Syrup, as prepared
on pages 23–24

Method

1 Wash and dry apricots. If large, cut in half; if small, leave whole. Prick surface with a darning needle to allow syrup to penetrate.

2 Follow steps 1–6 (page 25) and steps 1–4 (pages 25–26).

Cumquats

Ingredients

Cumquats, 8-10
Syrup, as prepared
on pages 23-4

Method

1 If cumquats are large, cut in half; if not, prepare as directed on page 23.

2 Place cumquats in syrup, set microwave on HIGH and boil for 6-8 minutes.

3 Follow steps 2-6 (page 25).

4 Dry cumquats on DEFROST for 15-20 minutes or until slightly sticky to touch.

5 Allow to stand on a cake cooler for 12 hours before storing (see page 23).

Ginger

Ingredients

Fresh ginger, 125 g
(4 oz)
Syrup, as prepared
on pages 23-24

Method

1 Peel or scrape outer skin from ginger. Cut into rounds 5 mm (¼ in) thick.

2 Place ginger in syrup, set microwave on HIGH and boil for 6-8 minutes or until slightly transparent.

3 Follow steps 2-6 (page 25).

4 Dry ginger on DEFROST for 10-15 minutes or until slightly sticky to touch.

5 Allow to stand on a cake cooler for 12 hours before storing (see page 23).

Grapes

Ingredients

Grapes, large, 24–30
Syrup, as prepared
on pages 23–24

Method

1 Use scissors to cut each grape from the bunch, leaving approximately 5 mm (¼ in) of stem attached to each grape. Wash gently in cold water and pat dry.

2 Prick each grape 5–6 times with a darning needle to prevent skins bursting during cooking and to allow syrup to penetrate.

3 Follow steps 1–6 (page 25) and steps 1–4 (pages 25–26).

Kiwi Fruit

Ingredients

Kiwi fruit, 4–5
Syrup, as prepared
on pages 23–24

Method

1 Peel and slice each kiwi fruit into 10-mm (½-in) slices.

2 Follow steps 1–6 (page 25) and steps 1–4 (pages 25–26).

Orange & Lemon Peel

Ingredients

Oranges, 2
Lemons, 2
Water, 500 ml
(2 cups), for
cooking peel
Syrup, as prepared
on pages 23–24
Soaking solution:
Water, 500 ml
(2 cups) for soaking
peel
Bicarbonate of soda,
1 teaspoon,
dissolved in 500 ml
(2 cups) cold water

Method

1 Remove zest from fruit with a vegetable peeler (do not peel into pith).

2 Cut peel into strips of approximately 5 cm (2 in) x 5 mm (¼ in).

3 To enhance colour soak peel for 20 minutes in soaking solution.

4 Drain and wash peel.

5 Place with water in a microwave-proof bowl and boil on high for 8–10 minutes.

6 Stand to cool approximately 20 minutes. Strain away water.

7 Place peel in syrup, set microwave on HIGH and boil for 5–6 minutes or until slightly transparent.

8 Follow steps 2–6 (page 25).

9 Dry peel on DEFROST for 10–12 minutes or until slightly sticky.

10 Allow to stand on a cake cooler for 12 hours before storing (see page 23).

Peaches

Ingredients

Peaches, yellow-
fleshed, 10-12
medium-sized

Syrup, as prepared
on pages 23-24

Method

1 Wash, dry and halve peaches. If fruit is very large, use only 6-8 and cut into quarters. Remove stones.

2 Follow steps 1-6 (page 25) and steps 1-4 (pages 25-26).

Pineapple

Ingredients

Pineapple, 1
medium-sized

Syrup, as prepared
on pages 23-24

Method

1 Remove all skin and eyes from pineapple.

2 Cut into 5-mm (¼-in) circles. Remove core. Use whole, halved or quartered.

3 Follow steps 1-6 (page 25) and steps 1-4 (pages 25-26).

Plums

Ingredients

Plums, 18-24

Syrup, as prepared
on pages 23-24

Method

1 Wash and dry plums. If large, cut in half; if small, leave whole. Prick surface with a darning needle to allow syrup to penetrate.

2 Follow steps 1-6 (page 25) and steps 1-4 (pages 25-26).

Chapter 3

Gourmet Jams and Chutneys

The recipes included here are slightly unusual. The fruits used are all readily available when in season but are rarely combined in such a delicious way.

The microwave method is quick and clean, and enhances the colour, flavour and nutrition of these preserves.

It is always advisable to store preserves for at least 3–4 weeks before use, thus enabling the flavours to mature.

Equipment

All types of jams, marmalades and chutneys require the same simple equipment. You will need:
- a large microwave-proof bowl with a cover
- a spoon, preferably wooden
- clean jars, free of chips, ridges or other imperfections, and covers or screw-top lids to fit.

Make sure the jars you intend to use fit in your oven with their lids on, if vacuum sealing.

Sterilising Your Equipment

1 Clean jars thoroughly in hot water, removing any adhesions with a bottle brush before sterilising.
2 Half-fill jars with cold water and cook on HIGH until water boils (approximately 2 minutes per jar).
3 Remove jars from microwave and fill the lids of the jars with the hot water.
4 Pour away water, allowing any excess to evaporate as the jars cool.

Warming the Jars

To achieve the best results, warm the jars just before filling them with cooked jam or chutney, as follows:
1 Cover bases of jars with water.
2 Place in microwave oven and cook on HIGH until water boils.
3 Pour off any excess water just before filling jars with fruit.

Setting Point

It is essential to test mixtures to make sure that setting point has been reached, otherwise the flavour, texture and colour of the product will be spoilt, making it

*These delicious chutneys add piquancy to
sandwiches and cold meats.*

*Home-made jam and scones are
hard to beat.*

unusable. In all jam-making, setting point is checked as follows:

1 Before preparing fruit, place an empty saucer in the refrigerator.
2 Remove bowl of cooked fruit from oven. (If you continue heating fruit while testing the sample, it may cook beyond setting point.)
3 Put a teaspoon of hot mixture on the cold saucer and let stand. When cool, the surface should crinkle when saucer is tilted slightly.
4 If test is negative, return bowl to oven and cook on HIGH for a few more minutes. Repeat test.

Vacuum Sealing Jams and Chutneys

Vacuum sealing expels air from filled jars and seals them. While it is not essential to vacuum seal jams and chutneys, the process will ensure the longest possible keeping time. Seal as follows:

1 Choose screw-top jars with built-in sealing rings.
2 After you fill the jars, lightly screw on their lids.
3 While filled jars are still hot, place them in oven, about 5 cm (2 in) apart and cook on MEDIUM–HIGH for 1–2 minutes. Remove jars from oven and place on a towel, several sheets of newspaper or a chopping board to prevent cracking. Screw lids down tightly, protecting your hands with an oven mitt or a towel, and let stand.
4 When cool, the lids will be slightly concave, showing that a vacuum seal has been achieved.

Storage

Store jams and chutneys in a cool, dark place. This retards the growth of mould. If mould does form, remove and discard it. Place remaining mixture in a microwave-proof bowl and cook on HIGH at boiling point for 2–3 minutes. Re-bottle in clean, warm, sterilised jars and vacuum seal.

Pectin and Fruit Acids

Pectin, a naturally occurring fruit acid, is a vital element in jams, without which they would not set. The highest quantities of pectin occur in fruits that are firm and just under-ripe (pectin in over-ripe fruit converts to sugar).

Fruits with high levels of acid are ideal, as the acid inhibits the growth of bacteria and prevents the formation of toxins. Natural fruit acids are also necessary because they draw out pectin, improve the flavour of the fruit and help prevent crystallisation.

If the fruit is over-ripe or naturally low in pectin or other fruit acids, lemon juice or citric acid must be added. The amounts required are specified in the recipes.

HIGH-PECTIN FRUITS	MEDIUM-PECTIN FRUITS	LOW-PECTIN FRUITS
cooking apples	apricots	bananas
crab apples	blackberries	ripe cherries
quinces	under-ripe berries	figs
citrus fruits:	loganberries	grapes
cumquats	greengage plums	peaches
mandarines	ripe plums	pears
grapefruit	pineapples	strawberries
lemons	rhubarb	melon
oranges	tamarillos	feijoas

Testing pectin content
Place a teaspoon of cooked or preserved fruit in 3 teaspoons of methylated spirits and leave for 2 minutes until mixture clots.

Large, firm clots indicate high pectin content. Medium-sized clots that are not so firm indicate medium pectin content. Weak, flabby clots indicate low pectin content.

Overcoming pectin deficiency

Sweet, over-ripe fruit and fruits low in pectin can be used in jams if one of the following steps is taken:

1 Add 2 tablespoons of lemon juice to every kilogram (4 cups) of fruit.
2 Add 1 teaspoon of citric acid to every kilogram (4 cups) of fruit.
3 Add commercially produced pectin, following the manufacturer's instructions.

Sugar

White granulated sugar is the most popular variety used to make jams, marmalades and chutneys. Sugar cubes can be used, but it is difficult to measure the exact proportion of sugar to fruit. Jam can crystallise if too much sugar is used, and it can ferment if too little is used.

Brown sugar can be used but it makes the preserves darker, so it should be used only for darker coloured fruits such as tamarillo and rhubarb.

Fruits with high or moderate pectin content (see page 34) require equal amounts of sugar and fruit pulp; for example, 1 cup of sugar to 1 cup of fruit.

Fruits with low pectin content require ¾ the amount of sugar to fruit pulp; for example, ¾ cup of sugar to 1 cup of fruit.

Feijoa & Lemon Jam

Ingredients

Feijoas, 1 kg (2 lb)
Lemons, 2, juice
and grated rind
Sugar, 750 g
(1½ lb)
Water, 375 ml
(1½ cups)

Method

1 Choose firm, unblemished feijoas which are slightly under-ripe. Cut away and discard any bruised areas.

2 Peel fruit and slice.

3 Place in a microwave-proof bowl with lemon rind, juice and water, cover and cook on HIGH until soft and pulpy (approximately 8–10 minutes).

4 Stir in remaining ingredients until sugar is fully dissolved.

5 Return mixture to microwave and cook uncovered on HIGH for approximately 20–25 minutes, until setting point has been reached (see page 32).

6 Skim jam to remove any scum.

7 Fill clean, warm, sterilised jars to the brim.

8 Vacuum seal according to directions on page 33.

9 Label and date jars.

10 Cool and store according to directions on page 33.

NOTE: Guavas may be used in place of feijoas.

Pineapple & Choko Jam

Ingredients

Pineapple, 1 small,
peeled and diced

Chokos, 1 kg (2 lb),
peeled and diced

Lemons, 3, juice
and grated rind

Sugar, 750 g
(1½ lb)

Whisky,
2 tablespoons

Method

1 Cut away and discard any bruises on the fruit and prepare as at left.

2 Place all ingredients in a microwave-proof bowl, cover and cook on HIGH for 4–6 minutes, or until boiling. Stir to dissolve sugar fully.

3 Return mixture to microwave and cook uncovered on HIGH for approximately 15–20 minutes, until setting point has been reached (see page 32).

4 Skim jam to remove any scum.

5 Fill clean, warm, sterilised jars to the brim.

6 Vacuum seal according to directions on page 33.

7 Label and date jars.

8 Cool and store according to directions on page 33.

Tamarillo & Apple Jam

Ingredients

Tamarillos, 1 kg
(2 lb)
Apples (Granny
Smith), 500 g (1 lb)
Sugar, 1 kg (2 lb)
Lemon juice,
2 tablespoons

Method

1 Cover tamarillos with boiling water and stand for 1 minute to remove skins. Cut up roughly.

2 Peel, core and grate apples.

3 Place all ingredients in a microwave-proof bowl, cover and cook on HIGH for 5-8 minutes, or until boiling. Stir to dissolve sugar fully.

4 Return mixture to microwave and cook uncovered on HIGH for approximately 18-25 minutes, until setting point has been reached (see page 32).

5 Skim jam to remove any scum.

6 Fill clean, warm, sterilised jars to the brim.

7 Vacuum seal according to directions on page 33.

8 Label and date jars.

9 Cool and store according to directions on page 33.

Rhubarb & Orange Jam

Ingredients

Rhubarb, 1 kg (2 lb)
Oranges, 2, juice
and grated rind
Sugar, 500 g (1 lb)
Water, ½ cup

Method

1 Wash rhubarb stalks and cut into small pieces.

2 Place all ingredients in a microwave-proof bowl, cover and cook on HIGH for 5–8 minutes, or until boiling. Stir to dissolve sugar fully.

3 Return mixture to microwave and cook uncovered on HIGH for approximately 15–20 minutes, until setting point has been reached (see page 32).

4 Skim jam to remove any scum.

5 Fill clean, warm, sterilised jars to the brim.

6 Vacuum seal according to directions on page 33.

7 Label and date jars.

8 Cool and store according to directions on page 33.

Honeydew Melon & Cumquat Jam

Ingredients

Honeydew melon,
1 kg (2 lb)

Cumquats, 1 kg
(2 lb)

Sugar, 1 kg
(2 lb)

Water, 1 cup

Method

1 Remove skin and seeds from melon and cut into small cubes. Place in a microwave-proof bowl, stir in sugar, cover and allow to stand overnight.

2 Cut washed cumquats into halves or quarters, place in a microwave-proof bowl, add water, cover and allow to stand overnight.

3 Next day, cook cumquats on HIGH for 5–8 minutes, or until boiling. Allow to cool.

4 Strain cumquat liquid into melon mixture and discard cumquats.

5 Cover this mixture and cook on HIGH until boiling. Stir to dissolve sugar fully.

6 Cook uncovered on HIGH for a further 15–20 minutes, until setting point has been reached (see page 32).

7 Skim jam to remove any scum.

8 Fill clean, warm, sterilised jars to the brim.

9 Vacuum seal according to directions on page 33.

10 Label and date jars.

11 Cool and store according to directions on page 33.

Rhubarb & Brandy Marmalade

Ingredients

Rhubarb, 1 kg (2 lb)

Raisins or sultanas, 250 g (½ lb)

Orange juice, ¼ cup

Lemon rind, shredded, 1 tablespoon

Cinnamon, ½ teaspoon

Whole cloves, 4

Sugar, 500 g (1 lb)

Brandy, ¼ cup

Method

1 Wash rhubarb stalks and cut into 2.5-cm (1-in) pieces. Place in a microwave-proof bowl, stir in sugar and allow to stand for 2-3 hours.

2 Add remaining ingredients, cover and cook on HIGH for 4-5 minutes, or until boiling. Stir to dissolve sugar fully.

3 Return mixture to microwave and cook uncovered on HIGH for approximately 20-25 minutes, until setting point has been reached (see page 32).

4 Skim marmalade to remove any scum.

5 Fill clean, warm, sterilised jars to the brim.

6 Vacuum seal according to directions on page 33.

7 Label and date jars.

8 Cool and store according to directions on page 33.

41

Peach, Apple &
Carrot Marmalade

Ingredients

Peaches (yellow-
fleshed), 500 g
(1 lb), peeled and
sliced thinly

Apples, 500 g (1 lb),
peeled and grated

Carrots, 500 g
(1 lb), grated

Lemon juice,
3 tablespoons

Sugar, 375 g (12 oz)

Method

1 Place all prepared ingredients in a
large microwave-proof bowl.

2 Cover and cook on HIGH for 4–5
minutes, or until boiling. Stir to dissolve
sugar fully.

3 Return mixture to microwave and
cook uncovered on HIGH for
approximately 18–20 minutes, until
setting point has been reached (see page
32).

4 Skim marmalade to remove any scum.

5 Fill clean, warm, sterilised jars to the
brim.

6 Vacuum seal according to directions
on page 33.

7 Label and date jars.

8 Cool and store according to directions
on page 33.

Lime & Mandarin Marmalade

Ingredients

Mandarins, 8
Limes, 2
Water, 4 cups
Sugar, 750 g
(1½ lb)

Method

1 Peel the fruit and shred skin or cut into fine strips.

2 Place peel in microwave-proof bowl, add 1 cup of water and cook on HIGH for approximately 5-6 minutes or until tender.

3 Slice fruit, place in a microwave-proof bowl, add remaining three cups of water and allow to stand overnight.

4 Cook on HIGH, uncovered, for 12-15 minutes or until fruit is tender.

5 Strain liquid away and discard fruit.

6 Add sugar and cooked peel to liquid, cover and cook on HIGH until boiling. Stir to dissolve sugar fully.

7 Return mixture to microwave and cook uncovered on HIGH for approximately 20-25 minutes, until setting point has been reached (see page 32).

8 Skim marmalade to remove any scum.

9 Fill clean, warm, sterilised jars to the brim.

10 Vacuum seal according to directions on page 33.

11 Label and date jars.

12 Cool and store according to directions on page 33.

Apple, Banana & Tomato Chutney

Ingredients

Apples (cooking),
1 kg (2 lb)

Tomatoes, ripe,
skinned 1 kg (2 lb)

Bananas, mashed,
2 cups

Sugar, 375 g (12 oz)

Vinegar, 1½ cups

Mustard seeds,
2 teaspoons

Chilli powder,
2 teaspoons

Turmeric,
1 teaspoon

Onions, large, 2

Salt, 1 teaspoon

Method

1 Peel, core and dice apples, and peel and dice onions. Cut tomatoes into small pieces.

2 Place all ingredients in a large microwave-proof bowl and cook on HIGH until boiling. Stir to dissolve sugar fully.

3 Return mixture to microwave and cook uncovered on HIGH for approximately 30–40 minutes, until mixture has thickened.

4 Fill clean, warm, sterilised jars to the brim.

5 Vacuum seal according to directions on page 33.

6 Label and date jars.

7 Cool and store according to directions on page 33.

Coconut & Gooseberry Chutney

Ingredients

Gooseberries, 1 kg
(2 lb)

Coconut, desiccated,
½ cup

Onions, large, 2

Raisins, 1 cup

Brown sugar, 375 g
(12 oz)

Vinegar, 1½ cups

Turmeric,
1 teaspoon

Cayenne,
½ teaspoon

Salt,
1 teaspoon

Method

1 Remove the stem and blossom ends of the gooseberries.

2 Peel and dice onions.

3 Place all ingredients in a microwave-proof bowl and cook on HIGH until boiling. Stir to dissolve sugar fully.

4 Return mixture to microwave and cook uncovered on HIGH for approximately 20–25 minutes, until gooseberries are pulpy and mixture has thickened.

5 Fill clean, warm, sterilised jars to the brim.

6 Vacuum seal according to directions on page 33.

7 Label and date jars.

8 Cool and store according to directions on page 33.

Capsicum Chutney

Ingredients

Capsicums, red, 6
Capsicums, green, 6
Onions, large, 2
Vinegar, 1½ cups
Sugar, 250 g (8 oz)
Salt, 1 teaspoon
Water, 1 cup

Method

1 Remove stems, veins and seeds from capsicums. Peel onions. Roughly chop capsicums and onions and place in a microwave-proof bowl.

2 Add water and cook on HIGH for approximately 6–8 minutes, until tender.

3 Drain off excess water.

4 Blend or mash vegetables together and add all other ingredients.

5 Cover and cook on HIGH until boiling. Stir to dissolve sugar fully.

6 Return mixture to microwave and cook uncovered on HIGH for approximately 15–20 minutes, until mixture has thickened.

7 Fill clean, warm, sterilised jars to the brim.

8 Vacuum seal according to directions on page 33.

9 Label and date jars.

10 Cool and store according to directions on page 33.

Mushroom & Choko Chutney

Ingredients

Mushrooms, 500 g
(1 lb)

Chokos, 4

Apples (Granny
Smith), 2

Capsicum (red or
green), 1

Vinegar, spiced,
½ cup

Sugar, 1 cup

Method

1 Peel mushrooms and remove stalks. Slice thinly. Peel, core and finely dice apples and chokos. Remove stem, veins and seeds from capsicum, and dice finely.

2 Place all ingredients in a large microwave-proof bowl.

3 Cover and cook on HIGH for approximately 2–3 minutes, until boiling. Stir to dissolve sugar fully.

4 Return mixture to microwave and cook uncovered on HIGH for approximately 25–35 minutes, until fruit is tender and mixture has thickened.

5 Fill clean, warm, sterilised jars to the brim.

6 Vacuum seal according to directions on page 33.

7 Label and date jars.

8 Cool and store according to directions on page 33.

Peach & Raisin Chutney

Ingredients

Peaches (yellow-fleshed), 1 kg (2 lb)

Apples (Granny Smith), 4

Raisins, 2 cups

Celery, 2 cups, chopped

Capsicum (red or green), 1

Vinegar, 2 cups

Sugar, 500 g (1 lb)

Method

1 Peel and stone peaches, and chop roughly. Peel, core and dice apples. Remove stem, veins and seeds from capsicum, and dice.

2 Place all ingredients in a large microwave-proof bowl.

3 Cover and cook on HIGH until boiling. Stir to dissolve sugar fully.

4 Return mixture to microwave and cook uncovered on HIGH for approximately 20–25 minutes, until fruit is tender and mixture has thickened.

5 Fill clean, warm, sterilised jars to the brim.

6 Vacuum seal according to directions on page 33.

7 Label and date jars.

8 Cool and store according to directions on page 33.

Save money by making your own glacé and crystallised fruit (pages 22–30).

Why not serve your own fruit liqueurs next time you have a dinner party?

Chapter 4

Fruit Liqueurs

Fruit liqueurs are made from natural fruit juices in an alcohol base. They are less expensive than the commercial equivalent and are fun to make, as well as being a source of pride as you sip away with friends after dinner and coffee.

To prepare a fruit liqueur the fruit is first cooked in the microwave for a few minutes to extract the juices and flavour, then sugar is added to sweeten, and finally the whole is combined with a spirit-based alcohol, for example brandy or gin.

The liqueur is allowed to infuse for up to a week before being strained and bottled. (Sterilise bottles by covering bottom with 2.5 cm (1 in) of water and cooking on HIGH until boiling. Pour boiling water into and over lids and let stand for 2–3 minutes. Drain water away.) A final maturing time of at least a month is necessary before serving, to achieve full bloom and flavour.

Because of their vivid colour and lustre, attractively bottled fruit liqueurs make a striking display in your cocktail bar or cabinet; and they make a most welcome gift.

Apricot Liqueur

Ingredients

Fresh apricots,
500 g (1 lb)

Ground allspice,
1 teaspoon

Sugar, 500 g (1 lb)

Dry white wine,
800 ml (3 cups)

Gin, 600 ml
(2½ cups)

Method

1 Choose well-ripened apricots and wash clean. Halve and remove stones.

2 Place fruit in a large microwave-proof bowl along with sugar, allspice and wine.

3 Cook on HIGH until boiling (approximately 5–6 minutes).

4 Stir to dissolve sugar. Cool. Add gin.

5 Cover bowl with a lid or plastic wrap and leave for 5–6 days to infuse.

6 Strain liqueur through a very fine strainer or muslin, squeezing out as much liquid as possible.

7 Fill clean, sterilised wine bottles, and cork or seal.

8 Store in a cool place for at least 1 month before serving.

Apricots in Liqueur

Ingredients

Fresh apricots, 1 kg
(2 lbs)
Apricot liqueur
(see opposite)

Method

1 Choose small-to-medium, firm apricots and wash clean.

2 Place whole fruit in a clean, sterilised jar.

3 Pour over apricot liqueur to within 1 cm (¹/₃ in) of the top of the jar. Cover with lid.

4 Store in a cool place for at least 1 month before using.

These apricots are delicious served with natural yoghurt or cream.

Strawberry or Blackberry Liqueur

Ingredients

Sugar, 500 g (1 lb)
Whole cloves, 6-8
Brandy, 200 ml
(¾ cup)
For berry juice:
Ripe berries, 1 kg
Water, 1 cup

Method

1 Place berries and water into a microwave-proof bowl.

2 Cook on HIGH for 5-8 minutes to extract juice.

3 Strain and measure up 1 litre (4 cups) of juice. (The remaining fruit can be chilled and used as a sweet.)

4 Place juice and sugar in a large microwave-proof bowl and cook on HIGH until boiling (approximately 5-6 minutes). Stir to dissolve sugar.

5 Add cloves and return syrup to microwave. Cook on HIGH a further 5-6 minutes.

6 Cool. Add brandy.

7 Cover bowl with a lid or plastic wrap and leave for 3 days to infuse.

8 Strain liqueur through a very fine strainer or muslin, squeezing out as much liquid as possible.

9 Fill clean, sterilised wine bottles, and cork or seal.

10 Store in a cool place for at least 1 month before serving.

Sultana Grapes in Berry Liqueur

Ingredients

Ripe grapes, 1 large
bunch

Berry liqueur
(see opposite)

Method

1 Using scissors cut each grape from
the bunch, leaving approximately 5 mm
(¼ in) of stem attached to each grape.
Wash gently in cold water and pat dry.

2 Place grapes carefully in clean,
sterilised jars.

3 Pour over berry liqueur to within
1 cm (¹/3 in) of the top of the jar. Cover
with lid.

4 Store in a cool place for at least 1
month before using.

Cherry Brandy

Ingredients

Cherries, 500 g
(1 lb)
Sugar, 125 g (4 oz)
Whole cloves, 3
Brandy, 850 ml
(3½ cups)

Method

1 Wash cherries and remove stones.

2 Place fruit and sugar in a microwave-proof bowl and cook on HIGH for 3-4 minutes or until cherries have softened slightly.

3 Remove from oven and allow to cool. Add cloves and brandy. Cover bowl with a lid or plastic wrap.

4 Allow to mature for 10-12 weeks.

5 Strain brandy through a very fine strainer or muslin, squeezing out as much liquid as possible.

6 Fill clean, sterilised wine bottles, and cork or seal.

7 Store in a cool place for at least 1 month before serving.

Peach Brandy

Ingredients

Yellow-fleshed peaches (clingstone or queen), 500 g (1 lb)

Sugar, 250 g (8 oz)

Ground nutmeg, ½ teaspoon

Brandy, 600 ml (2½ cups)

Method

1 Leaving skins on, wash peaches, halve and remove stones. Slice roughly.

2 Place fruit, sugar and nutmeg in a microwave-proof bowl and cook on HIGH for 2–3 minutes.

3 Remove from oven and allow to cool. Add brandy. Cover bowl with a lid or plastic wrap.

4 Allow to mature for 10–14 days.

5 Strain brandy through a very fine strainer or muslin, squeezing out as much liquid as possible.

6 Fill clean, sterilised wine bottles, and cork or seal.

7 Store in a cool place for at least 1 month before serving.

Raspberry Gin

Ingredients

Raspberries, fresh or
preserved, 350 g
(12 oz)

Sugar, 90 g (3 oz)
Gin, 500 ml
(2 cups)

Method

1 If fresh, choose firm, unblemished raspberries. Hull, wash and dry.

2 Place fruit, sugar and gin in a glass container or bottle, stir, and seal with plastic wrap or a cork.

3 Allow to mature in a cool place for at least 3 months, occasionally stirring or shaking gently.

4 Strain gin through a very fine strainer or muslin. Fill clean, sterilised wine bottles, and cork or seal.

The leftover raspberries are great as a dessert served with ice-cream.

Crystallised Fruit in Cognac

A single crystallised fruit or a combination of fruits in liqueur is delicious served with cream or ice-cream on a special occasion.

Ingredients

Whole pieces of crystallised fruit (see Chapter 2)

Cognac

Method

1 Clean and sterilise suitably sized jars and lids.

2 Fill jars with crystallised fruit.

3 Pour over cognac to within 1 cm (1/3 in) of the top of the jar. Cover with lid.

4 Store in a cool place for at least 1 month before using.

Chapter 5

Fruit Sorbets

Sorbet is a frozen mixture made from sweetened fruit pureé, fruit juices or milk, egg whites and sometimes gelatine, depending on the acidity of the fruit.

Traditionally sorbet has been served at formal dinners, to clean the palate between the first and the main courses. These days it is more commonly served at informal dinners as part of a refreshing dessert, along with cold fruit — especially appealing in warm weather.

It is important to taste the sorbet before freezing, so that more sugar can be added if necessary.

Sorbet is served in a glass or a sweets dish as it is too soft to mould.

Banana Sorbet

Ingredients

Mashed banana,
2 cups
Lemon juice, ¼ cup
Sugar, ½ cup
Egg white, 1
Milk, 2 cups

Method

1 Purée banana by blending or passing through a coarse sieve. Add lemon juice and sugar.

2 Beat egg white until stiff, fold into banana and slowly stir in milk.

3 Freeze in freezer trays for 1 hour. Remove from trays and beat until smooth. Return mixture to trays and refreeze until just firm.

Cherry Sorbet

Ingredients

Fresh cherries,
2½ cups
Sugar, ¾ cup
Almond essence,
¼ teaspoon
Milk, 3 cups

Method

1 Wash and pit cherries, blend to a pulp before measuring. Make up 2½ cups of fruit and juice together.

2 Add sugar to pulp, place in a microwave-proof bowl, cover and heat on HIGH until boiling (approximately 2–3 minutes).

3 Remove and stir to dissolve sugar.

4 Add almond essence and milk.

5 Freeze in freezer trays for 1 hour before serving.

Mango Sorbet

Ingredients

Large, ripe mangoes,
2
OR
Mango puree, 1 cup
Sugar, ½ cup
Water, 375 ml
(1½ cups)
Lemon juice, ⅓ cup
Egg whites, 2

Method

1 Skin mangoes and remove flesh from seed. Purée flesh by blending until smooth.

2 Combine sugar and water in microwave-proof bowl. Heat on HIGH until boiling (approximately 2–3 minutes).

3 Remove and stir to dissolve sugar.

4 Return syrup to oven and boil on HIGH for a further 5–6 minutes. Cool.

5 Stir in mango purée and lemon juice.

6 Freeze in freezer trays until just firm, for approximately 1 hour. Remove from trays and beat until smooth.

7 Beat egg whites until stiff and fluffy, and fold into mango mixture until smooth.

8 Return mixture to trays and refreeze.

Orange Sorbet

Ingredients

Fresh orange juice,
2 cups
Sugar, 1½ cups
Water, 250 ml
(1 cup)
Lemon juice,
3 tablespoons
Egg whites, 2

Method

1 Combine sugar and water in microwave-proof bowl. Heat on HIGH for 2 minutes.

2 Remove and stir to dissolve sugar. Cool.

3 Beat egg whites until stiff and gradually beat in cooled syrup, lemon and orange juice.

4 Pour into freezer trays and freeze for approximately 1 hour, or until partially frozen.

5 Remove from trays and spoon into a bowl. Beat until smooth but not fully melted.

6 Return mixture to trays and refreeze.

Grapefruit or a combination of grapefruit and orange juice can be used in place of orange and lemon juices.

Pineapple Sorbet

Ingredients

Crushed pineapple,
2 cups

Sugar, 1 cup

Water or pineapple
juice, 2 cups

Cream, 2 cups

Method

1 Place sugar and water in a microwave-proof bowl. Cover and heat on HIGH until boiling. Boil for 2 minutes.

2 Remove and cool.

3 Add all other ingredients and mix together.

4 Freeze in freezer trays for 1 hour.

5 Remove from trays and beat until smooth.

6 Return mixture to trays and refreeze.

Rhubarb & Strawberry Sorbet

Ingredients

Strawberries,
2½ cups

Cooked rhubarb,
2 cups

Lemon juice,
2 tablespoons

Sugar, 1½ cups

Cream, ¾ cup

Method

1 Wash berries, hull and mash. Purée rhubarb and berries by blending or pressing through a coarse sieve.

2 Stir in all other ingredients.

3 Freeze in freezer trays until just firm (approximately 1 hour).

4 Just before serving, scrape up thin layers of the mixture with a large spoon. Place in a bowl and stir until smooth. Serve immediately.

Chapter 6

Fruit Tarts

The dried fruit fillings in this chapter will enable you to make a variety of tarts. With the help of your microwave they are quick and easy to make and, if vacuum-sealed, will keep for many months. Once opened, however, a jar of these fillings must be refrigerated and used within a few days. For this reason I suggest using small recyclable jars, which will hold just enough for one tart.

Although commercially-made pie shells are readily available, I've included a recipe for champagne pastry, for those of you who like to make your own.

*Add your own finishing touches to the dried
fruit tarts in this chapter.*

Refreshing fruit sorbets (pages 58–63)
and plum pudding ice-cream (page 88).

To Vacuum Seal

Vacuum sealing expels air from filled jars and seals them for long-term storage.

1 Choose jars that have metal screw tops with built-in sealing rings.
2 After you fill the jars, lightly screw on their lids.
3 While filled jars are still warm, place them in oven, no closer than 3 cm (1¼ in) apart, with a maximum of 4 sealed jars at a time. Cook according to the following chart:

JAR SIZE	OVEN SETTING	COOKING TIME
200–300 ml	medium–high	1½ mins
350–450 ml	medium–high	2 mins
500–650 ml	medium–high	3 mins

NOTE: Times apply to one jar only. For every additional jar add 1 minute's extra cooking time.

4 Remove jars from oven and place on a towel, several sheets of newspaper or a chopping board to prevent cracking. Screw lids down tightly, protecting your hands with an oven mitt or a towel, and let stand.
5 When cool, the lids will be slightly concave, showing that a vacuum seal has been achieved.
6 Store in a cool, dark place until ready for use. Once opened, store in the refrigerator for no more than a week.

Champagne Pastry Shell

This biscuit pastry contains less fat than many other pastries and is therefore particularly suited to microwave cooking.

The secret to biscuit pastry is to knead it well before rolling, so that it keeps its shape during cooking.

Remember that this pastry does not brown in the microwave.

Ingredients

Self-raising flour,
175 g (6 oz)

Cornflour, 90 g
(3 oz)

Butter or margarine,
90 g (3 oz)

Sugar, 60 g (2 oz)

Egg yolks, 2

Milk, 3 tablespoons

Method

1 Set microwave on HIGH and soften butter or margarine for approximately 30 seconds.

2 Add sugar and egg yolks and beat until creamy.

3 Add flours and milk. Mix to a firm dough. If mixture is soft place in refrigerator for ½ hour or until firm.

4 Place dough on a lightly floured board and knead well for 2–3 minutes.

5 Roll out to approximately 5 mm (¼ in) thick and line a 22-cm (9-in) microwave-proof pie plate.

6 Crimp edges and prick pastry base well with a fork.

7 Set microwave on HIGH and cook pastry shell for 4–6 minutes.

8 Remove and allow to cool.

9 Fill with your favourite fruit filling.

Date Tart

Ingredients

Dates, stoned and chopped, 2 cups
Sugar, ¼ cup
Water, ½ cup
Butter, 2 tablespoons
Lemon juice, ¼ cup
Champagne pastry shell (see page 66)
Decoration:
Crushed nuts, shredded coconut or whipped cream

Method

1 Place dates and water in a microwave-proof bowl. Cover, cook on MEDIUM-HIGH until tender (about 6–8 minutes).

2 Stir in sugar, butter and lemon juice.

3 Cool slightly.

4 If not using immediately, bottle, vacuum seal and store as instructed on page 65.

5 Otherwise, spoon into pastry shell.

6 Cool further and top with crushed nuts, shredded or desiccated coconut, or whipped cream before serving.

Date & Coconut Tart

Ingredients

Date filling as prepared on page 73, ½ quantity

Champagne pastry shell as prepared (see page 66)

Topping:
Egg whites, 2
Sugar, 60 g (2 oz)
Desiccated coconut, ½ cup

Method

1 Mix all topping ingredients thoroughly.

2 Spread date filling over base of pastry. Cover with topping.

3 Set microwave on HIGH and cook for 5–6 minutes.

4 Serve hot or cold with cream or ice-cream.

NOTE: Other fillings may be substituted.

Dried Apple & Banana Tart

Ingredients

Dried apples, finely chopped, 1½ cups

Fresh, mashed bananas, 1½ cups

Sugar, ¼ cup

Water, ½ cup

Vanilla essence, 1 teaspoon

Champagne pastry shell (see page 66)

Decoration: Nuts, shredded coconut or whipped cream.

Method

1 Place dried, chopped apples and water in a microwave-proof bowl. Cover, cook on MEDIUM-HIGH until tender (about 8–10 minutes).

2 Stir in sugar. Cool.

3 Mix mashed banana into cooled apples; add vanilla.

4 If not using immediately, bottle, vacuum seal and store as instructed on page 65.

5 Otherwise, spoon into pastry shell. Cool further and top with crushed nuts, shredded or desiccated coconut, or whipped cream before serving.

Dried Apricot Tart

Ingredients

Dried apricots,
chopped,
2 cups

Sugar, ¼ cup

Water, ½ cup

Almond essence,
½ teaspoon

Apricot liqueur
(See page 50),
1 tablespoon
(optional)

Champagne pastry
shell (see page 66)

Decoration:
Crushed nuts,
shredded coconut or
whipped cream

Method

1 Place dried apricots and water in a microwave-proof bowl. Cover, cook on MEDIUM-HIGH until fruit is tender (about 8–10 minutes).

2 Stir sugar into hot fruit. Allow to cool.

3 Add almond essence and apricot liqueur.

4 If not using immediately, bottle, vacuum seal and store as instructed on page 65.

5 Otherwise, spoon into pastry shell. Cool further and top with crushed nuts, shredded or desiccated coconut, or whipped cream before serving.

Dried Apricot & Chocolate Tart

Ingredients

Crust:

Chocolate-flavoured biscuits, 125 g (4 oz)

Butter or margarine, 60 g (2 oz)

Cocoa, 1 tablespoon

Filling:

Dried apricots, 180 g (6 oz)

Water, ¾ cup

Orange juice, ¾ cup

Apricot liqueur (See page 50), 2 tablespoons

Evaporated milk, chilled, 1 x 375-ml can

Gelatine, 1 tablespoon

Warm water, 2 tablespoons

Garnish:

Cream for whipping

Chocolate for grating

Method

Crust:

1 Crush biscuits finely. Set oven on HIGH and melt butter or margarine with cocoa in a microwave-proof bowl for 1–1½ minutes.

2 Stir and pour over crushed biscuits. Mix well together.

3 Press mixture onto base of an 18-cm (8-in) springform pan.

4 Chill.

Filling:

1 Place dried apricots, orange juice, water and liqueur in a microwave-proof bowl and cover.

2 Cook on MEDIUM-HIGH until apricots are tender (approximately 12–15 minutes). Cool.

3 Blend mixture to a smooth purée in a food processor. Dissolve gelatine in warm water and heat on HIGH until boiling (approximately 20 seconds). Stir into apricot mixture.

4 Beat chilled evaporated milk until very thick. Add apricots, purée and beat thoroughly.

5 Pour over biscuit base and level out surface.

6 Decorate with whipped cream and grated chocolate.

NOTE: Other dried fruits may be substituted for apricots.

Dried Apricot & Coffee Tart

Ingredients

Topping:
Plain flour, 90 g (3 oz)

Butter or margarine, 450 g (1 ½ oz)

Sugar, 30 g (1 oz)

Instant coffee powder, 1 teaspoon

Filling:
Dried apricot filling as prepared on page 70

Champagne pastry shell (see page 66)

Method

1 Mix together all dry ingredients. Using fingertips rub in butter or margarine until the mixture resembles breadcrumbs.

2 Spread apricot filling over base of pastry. Cover with topping.

3 Set microwave on HIGH and cook for 5-6 minutes.

4 Serve hot or cold with cream or ice-cream.

NOTE: Other fillings may be substituted.

Dried Fig Tart

Ingredients

Dried figs, chopped,
2 cups

Sugar, ¼ cup

Water, ¼ cup

Lemon juice, ¼ cup

Champagne pastry
shell (see page 66)

Decoration:
Crushed nuts,
shredded coconut or
whipped cream

Method

1 Place dried figs and water in a microwave-proof bowl. Cover, cook on MEDIUM-HIGH until tender (about 8–10 minutes).

2 Stir in sugar and lemon juice.

3 Cool slightly.

4 If not using immediately, bottle, vacuum seal and store as instructed on page 65.

5 Otherwise, spoon into pastry shell.

6 Cool further and top with crushed nuts, shredded or desiccated coconut, or whipped cream before serving.

Dried Fig & Walnut Tart

Ingredients

Dried figs, finely chopped, 1 cup

Walnuts, chopped, ½ cup

Water, ¼ cup

Golden syrup, ¼ cup

Sugar, ¼ cup

Lemon juice, ¼ cup

Champagne pastry shell (see page 66)

Decoration:
Crushed walnuts

Method

1 Place dried figs and water in a microwave-proof bowl. Cover, cook on MEDIUM-HIGH until tender (about 8–10 minutes).

2 Stir in all other ingredients.

3 Cool slightly.

4 If not using immediately, bottle, vacuum seal and store as instructed on page 65.

5 Otherwise, spoon into pastry shell.

6 Cool further and top with crushed walnuts. Serve with whipped cream.

Mixed Dried Fruit Tart

Ingredients

Mixed dried citrus
peel, ¼ cup

Apples, dried, ½ cup

Apricots, dried,
½ cup

Figs, dried, ½ cup

Mango, dried,
½ cup

Sultana grapes,
dried, ½ cup

Brown sugar, ¾ cup

Water, 1¼ cups

Cherry brandy (See
page 54), ¼ cup
(optional)

Ground cinnamon
and nutmeg,
½ teaspoon

Decoration:
Crushed nuts,
shredded coconut or
whipped cream

Method

1 Place all ingredients except cherry
brandy into a microwave-proof bowl,
cover and cook on MEDIUM-HIGH until
fruit is tender (approximately 10–12
minutes).

2 Allow to cool.

3 Stir in cherry brandy.

4 If not using immediately, bottle,
vacuum seal and store as instructed on
page 65.

5 Otherwise, spoon into pastry shell.

6 Cool further and top with crushed
nuts, shredded or desiccated coconut, or
whipped cream before serving.

Prune Tart

Ingredients

Prunes, finely chopped, 1½ cups

Walnuts, chopped, ½ cup

Butter or margarine, 2 tablespoons

Water, ¼ cup

Sugar, ½ cup

Ground cinnamon, 1 teaspoon

Champagne pastry shell (see page 66)

Method

1 Place prunes and water into a microwave-proof bowl. Cover and cook on MEDIUM-HIGH until fruit is tender (approximately 8–10 minutes).

2 Stir sugar and butter or margarine into hot fruit.

3 Allow to cool.

4 Stir in nuts and cinnamon.

5 Cool slightly.

6 If not using immediately, bottle, vacuum seal and store as instructed on page 65.

7 Otherwise, spoon into pastry shell. Serve with cream.

Raisin Tart

Ingredients

Raisins, chopped,
2 cups

Butter or margarine,
1 tablespoon

Water, ½ cup

Sugar, ½ cup

Champagne pastry
shell (see page 66)

Decoration:
Pecan nuts or
walnuts

Method

1 Place raisins and water into a microwave-proof bowl. Cover, cook on MEDIUM-HIGH until tender (about 6–8 minutes).

2 Stir in all other ingredients.

3 Cool slightly.

4 If not using immediately, bottle, vacuum seal and store as instructed on page 65.

5 Otherwise, spoon into pastry shell.

6 Cool further and top with pecan nuts or walnuts. Serve with whipped cream.

Chapter 7

$\mathcal{F}$ruit Ice-creams

Ice-cream is one of the world's most popular and most versatile desserts. The fruit ice-creams in this chapter would enhance a variety of other desserts but are delicious enough to serve on their own, particularly the superb Plum Pudding Ice-cream, the Fruit Mince Ice-cream and the delicate Peach and Almond Ice-cream.

The purées used in these recipes can be made from dried, preserved or fresh fruits (see directions on page 80).

These days ice-cream is simple to make. The following hints will guarantee good results.

Helpful Hints

1 The addition of too much sugar or sweetener can cause ice-cream to freeze more slowly or not at all, so measure ingredients carefully.
2 Beat cream only until it forms soft peaks. If beaten too thickly it will be difficult to incorporate into the other ingredients to achieve a smooth finish. Also, over-beaten cream can give the ice-cream an unpleasant buttery flavour.
3 A snap-freeze gives the best results and helps to eliminate the formation of icicles throughout the ice-cream.
4 It is better to use puréed fruit rather than whole, as it will give a more even distribution of flavour and reduce the possibility of crystallisation.

Fruit Purée

Fruit purée is cooked fruit either forced through a sieve, blended or mashed into a fine pulp. The thickness of the purée depends on the amount of water or liquid present before blending. Purée for the ice-creams included here should not be too thin, so take care to use little water when cooking the fruit.

Dried Fruit Purée

Chop 1 cup dried fruit into small pieces. Place in a microwave-proof bowl. Add ¼ cup water or fruit juice and cover. Cook on MEDIUM-HIGH until soft (approximately 8–10 minutes). Stir in required sugar until dissolved. Purée.

Preserved Fruit Purée

Drain away syrup or liquid from fruit and refrigerate for further use. Place fruit in a microwave-proof bowl, cover and cook on HIGH for 1–2 minutes. Taste and sweeten if required. Purée.

NOTE: Preserved bananas do not require cooking.

Fresh Fruit Purée

Prepare fruit by peeling and removing core or stones. Halve or quarter. Place in a microwave-proof bowl. Add ¼ cup water or fruit juice and cover. Cook on MEDIUM-HIGH until soft — approximately 5–6 minutes per 500 g (1 lb) of fruit. Stir in required sugar (approximately ¼ cup) until dissolved. Purée.

NOTE: Fresh bananas do not require cooking.

Apricot Ice-cream

Ingredients

Apricot purée (See page 80), 1½ cups
Gelatine, 1 teaspoon
Water, ¼ cup
Sugar, ¼ cup
Cream, 1 cup
Almond essence, ½ teaspoon

Method

1 Soak gelatine in water for 2–3 minutes.

2 Mix with apricot purée and sugar. Heat on HIGH to boiling point (approximately 2 minutes). Stir to dissolve sugar.

3 Cool and pour into freezer trays. Freeze for approximately 1 hour or until half-frozen.

4 Whip cream until soft peaks are formed. Fold into purée along with almond essence.

5 Return mixture to freezer trays. Freeze until firm. Serve.

6 Accompany with preserved fruit of your choice.

NOTE: *Plum, peach or pear purée can be substituted for apricot.*

Banana Ice-cream

Ingredients

Banana purée (See page 80), 2 cups
Sweetened condensed milk, 1 cup
Water, ¼ cup
Cream, 1 cup
Lemon juice, 2 teaspoons

Method

1 Mix together condensed milk, banana purée water and lemon juice.

2 Pour into freezer trays and freeze for approximately 1 hour or until half frozen.

3 Whip cream until soft peaks are formed. Fold into purée.

4 Return mixture to freezer trays. Freeze until firm. Serve.

5 Accompany with preserved fruit of your choice.

Chocolate Banana Ice-cream

Ingredients

Banana purée (See page 80), 1 cup
Cocoa, 2 tablespoons
Milk, 2 ½ cups
Sweetened condensed milk, ½ cup
Gelatine, 2 teaspoons
Water, ¼ cup
Cream, 1 cup
Powdered milk, 4 tablespoons

Method

1 Soak gelatine in cold water for 2-3 minutes and add cocoa.

2 Heat on HIGH until gelatine has dissolved (approximately 1-2 minutes). Do not stir.

3 Beat all other ingredients together and stir in gelatine and cocoa mixture.

4 Pour into freezer trays and freeze for approximately 1 hour.

5 Turn out into a bowl, beat well and stir in banana purée.

6 Pour mixture into freezer trays. Freeze until firm. Serve.

Fig & Honey Ice-cream

Ingredients

Fig purée (See page 80), 1 cup
Honey, ¼ cup
Junket tablet, 1
Water, 1 tablespoon
Cream, 1 cup
Milk, 1 cup

Method

1 Crush junket tablet and dissolve in cold water.

2 Warm milk and honey on HIGH until blood temperature is reached (approximately 1–1½ minutes). Stir into junket and water. Leave until mixture is firm (about 10 minutes). Cool in refrigerator for about 30 minutes.

3 Whip cream until it forms soft peaks. Fold into junket.

4 Pour into freezer trays and freeze for approximately 1 hour or until mixture is partly frozen.

5 Turn out into a bowl, add fig purée and beat lightly until smooth but not melted.

6 Pour mixture into freezer trays. Freeze until firm. Serve.

Fruit Mince Ice-cream

Ingredients

Fruit mince, 1 cup

Water, ½ cup

Sweetened condensed milk, ⅔ cup

Cream, 1 cup

Vanilla, or cherry brandy (See page 54), 2 teaspoons

Method

1 Place fruit mince and water in a microwave-proof bowl. Heat on HIGH for 1–2 minutes or until just below boiling point.

2 Stir in condensed milk and allow mixture to cool.

3 Whip cream until it forms soft peaks. Fold into cold fruit mixture. Add cherry brandy or vanilla.

4 Pour into freezer trays and freeze for approximately 1 hour or until partly frozen.

5 Turn out into a bowl and beat until smooth but not melted.

6 Return to freezer trays. Freeze until firm. Serve.

Peach & Almond Ice-cream

Ingredients

Peach purée (See page 80), 1 cup

Almond pieces, ¼ cup

Sugar, ¼ cup

Gelatine, 2 teaspoons

Fresh cream, 1 cup

Water, ¼ cup

Almond essence, ½ teaspoon

Method

1 Soak gelatine in water for 2-3 minutes.

2 Heat peach purée on HIGH for 1½ minutes. Stir in sugar and gelatine/water until dissolved. Cool.

3 Pour into freezer trays and freeze for approximately 1 hour or until mixture is partly frozen.

4 Turn out into a bowl, beat lightly until smooth but not melted.

5 Whip cream until it forms soft peaks, fold into cold mixture along with almond pieces and essence.

6 Pour mixture into freezer trays. Freeze until firm. Serve.

Pineapple & Marshmallow Ice-cream

Ingredients

Pineapple purée (See page 80), 1 cup

Marshmallows, 125g (4 oz)

Milk, 1 cup

Fresh cream, 1 cup

Method

1 Cut marshmallows into small pieces and place in microwave-proof bowl. Cover with milk.

2 Heat on HIGH for 1½ minutes. Stir to dissolve marshmallows. Cool until a syrup consistency is reached.

3 Whip cream until it forms soft peaks and fold into cold mixture.

4 Pour into freezer trays and freeze for approximately 1 hour or until mixture is partly frozen.

5 Turn out into a bowl and stir in pineapple purée until smooth.

6 Pour mixture into freezer trays and chill until firm. Serve.

Plum Pudding Ice-cream

Ingredients

Fresh cream,
2½ cups

Icing sugar, 180 g
(6 oz)

Mixed dried fruits,
1½ cup

Egg whites, 4

Slivered almonds,
60 g (2 oz)

Mixed spice,
2 teaspoons

Cinnamon,
1 teaspoon

Nutmeg, 1 teaspoon

Brandy or vanilla,
2 teaspoons

Cocoa, 1 tablespoon

Hot water,
2 tablespoons

Method

1 Chop dried fruits finely. Mix in spices, almonds, and brandy or vanilla and allow to stand for 2-3 hours.

2 Whip cream until stiff and stir in half the icing sugar.

3 In another bowl beat egg whites stiffly and fold in remaining icing sugar.

4 Gently fold together the cream and egg mixtures. Add fruit and the cocoa dissolved in the hot water.

5 Pour into freezer trays or an aluminium pudding mould lined with foil.

6 Freeze overnight or until firm.

Conversion Table

Abbreviations

g	=	gram(s)
kg	=	kilogram(s)
mm	=	millimetre(s)
cm	=	centimetre(s)
oz	=	ounce(s)
lb	=	pound(s)
in	=	inch(es)

Liquid measures

250 ml	=	½ pint	=	1 cup
375 ml	=	¾ pint	=	1½ cups
500 ml	=	1 pint	=	2 cups
1 litre	=	2 pints	=	4 cups

Dry weights

30 g	=	1 oz
60 g	=	2 oz
90 g	=	3 oz
125 g	=	4 oz
250 g	=	8 oz
500 g	=	1 lb
1 kg	=	2 lbs

Measures

5 mm	=	¼ in
1 cm	=	1/3 in
2.5 cm	=	1 in
5 cm	=	2 in

Index